BLUFF Y[...]
THE OCCULT

ALEXANDER C. RAE

RAVETTE BOOKS

Published by Ravette Books Limited
3 Glenside Estate, Star Road,
Partridge Green, Horsham,
Sussex RH13 8RA
(0403) 710392

Series Editor – Anne Tauté

Cover design – Jim Wire
Typesetting – Input Typesetting Ltd.
Printing & Binding – Cox & Wyman Ltd
Production – Oval Projects Ltd.

The Bluffer's Guides are based on
an orginal idea by Peter Wolfe.

For the objects on the cover, grateful thanks are due to:

Bruce Robertson, for the use of his skull.

CONTENTS

INTRODUCTION

There is no area of human endeavour better suited to the art of bluffing than the occult sciences. For a start 90 per cent of the 'experts' on the subject spend the whole of their lives bluffing. The other 10 per cent are loonies and better kept clear of. Knowing that the 'expert' is bluffing can help you enormously, although it is wise not to push things too far. There is just the chance that he really could turn you into a frog.

This doesn't mean that you can entirely make it up as you go along, although there is no other area where you can get by on fewer facts as long as you have a quick brain and a good imagination. But remember at some time or another you are likely to come up against a master-bluffer and if you are not careful, he will recognise the technique and ruthlessly expose your ignorance.

Still, once you have mastered a few techniques and learnt certain key words you can pass yourself off as a high ranking adept successfully enough that even if your opponent thinks you are bluffing he will not push his luck – just in case you turn him into a frog.

At the end of the day you always have the last resort of covering your ignorance by claiming that you cannot disclose any further information because of some binding vows you took to an unnamed but extremely powerful cult, or else that the information asked of you cannot be disclosed to the ears of the profane. This is the equivalent of the old "Well to tell you the truth I am a CIA agent" technique which should only be used if all else fails. It can just work if the listeners are gullible enough, but it might be worth practising leaving rooms with as much dignity as you can muster while everyone is laughing at you – or else really come up with a technique for turning disbelievers into frogs.

BASIC RULES

A New Image

If you are really going to take occult bluffing seriously the most important factor in achieving credibility is getting the image right. Stand in front of the mirror for a few hours every night perfecting a slightly mad, hypnotic stare. Take either Aleister Crowley or Charles Manson as your model. Both spent a lot of time in front of the mirror perfecting theirs.

Dress in black and even wear a long cloak if you think you can get away with it. Be photographed in long robes covered in strange Astrological symbols and magical accoutrements (Eliphas Levi started the trend and of course Crowley did it to death). However it is wise not to push these too hard. Let them be discovered by accident – don't show them to everyone in the pub along with your holiday snaps from Ibiza.

A change of name is often useful. Grand Master of the Order of the Black Rose Albert Higgins just doesn't sound right somehow. Something exotic and foreign is ideal and an obscure title is a real clincher if you can carry it off. There is a long tradition amongst occultists to claim to be Scottish chieftains (MacGregor-Mathers and Aleister Cowley both tried it) and it seems to work even if you have never been north of the Watford Gap. On the other hand a dukedom or countship from some vague Eastern European country might be more practical. It is easier to pass off the phony accent as authentic and you are less likely to meet another Lithuanian Compte who could expose your little peccadillo.

It almost goes without saying that a change of address is needed. Don't go to the pub where you have been going every Saturday for the last 25 years and suddenly insist that your name is really Nikolai Slimi-vitch, le Duc de Milton Keynes.

Similarly a change of location gives you a romantic mystery about you that can work wonders. A delightfully vague history is almost a pre-requisite for the successful occultist. One or two tips though. Don't get the newsletter from your old Pigeon Fanciers Club forwarded to your new address, and make sure you move to somewhere you know absolutely no-one – especially relatives. Nothing can kill a reputation for mystery like an aging aunt telling everyone how she remembers you when you were on your potty.

Secret Knowledge

The important thing to remember when building a reputation for occult knowledge is that you have to give the impression of having some knowledge and it has to be occult. There are various ways of doing this.

One is to hint darkly that you have knowledge but you're not telling anyone about it because it's a secret. You need to be good to get away with that one.

Far better is telling everyone what your secret knowledge is but in such an obscure, long winded and downright confusing way that no-one realises you are talking nonsense. This is the way that has been chosen by most occultists throughout history. People will seldom admit outright that they think you're talking nonsense, especially if you make it sound impressive and throw in a few uncheckable facts and Latin quotes.

Even more important than Latin quotes is the need to get a pedigree. You really want your knowledge passed down to you from a secret society, or better still, a series of societies. This is much easier in occultism than in any other field of human knowledge.

Throughout history there have been a succession of mysterious bodies involved in occult matters. By their very nature they kept these interests secret. As a lot of them ended up getting burnt at the stake it would seem they should have kept their views even more secret.

This of course makes them ideal for using as the guardians that carefully nurtured this knowledge through trial and tribulation so that they could hand it on to you. They can't turn round and deny it.

First decide on where the knowledge started from. There are several favourites for this. Then pick your historic route trying to keep it pretty logical. Don't suggest that the Cathars passed it on to the North American Shamans before America was discovered, for instance.

If you want to do a bit of research you can take any of these bodies and find out the pedigree they invented for themselves. These usually go back to Adam at least and are pretty impressive.

It is perhaps possible to claim that your Secret Doctrine has been handed down from a race of super-beings that inhabited Atlantis, as there is no way anyone can positively refute it, but it is inclined to get you labelled as a crank.

Far better to pick a more sensible source of knowledge, like the Egyptians, Druids, any of the archangels or anyone mentioned in Genesis.

FAVOURED SOURCES

Druids

There are two things that people know about Druids:

1. They built Stonehenge
2. They probably invented the alarm clock (how else could they get up to see dawn on the Vernal Equinox).

The problem is that experts now think they didn't build Stonehenge, but it was some vague group before them that died out through sheer frustration at trying to get the roof on.

Seldom will you come across a group with such advantages for the bluffer. A religion that everyone has heard of and yet at least half of the known information is totally inaccurate. Ideal for being an expert on.

The Druids were considerate enough to develop the idea of 'the oral tradition', developed mainly through embarrassment at not being able to do joined-up writing. So what is actually left of their culture is a few nicely carved artifacts, and whatever you want to make up yourself.

It is handy to know that Druid means 'knowledge of the oak tree' which interestingly enough was the whole point of Frazer's *The Golden Bough* which took 12 volumes to find out what *The Golden Bough* was. Those who peeked at the end know the answer is 'mistletoe'.

For the bluffer, the Druids have another perfect advantage in that no-one really knows what period of history they covered; some bluffers have been using them as retainers of secret knowledge up to the middle of the 10th century, but this obviously has to handled with panache.

Qabalism

Knowing the word qabalism is essential, mainly because it is one of the few words you can lay down in Scrabble if you have a Q and no U. However, for the occult bluffer it is an ideal subject. Anyone who is partially in the know will have heard of it, but virtually no-one will know enough to argue with anything you say.

First of all be sure to pronounce it correctly. Most people will pronounce and even spell it Cabalism or Kabalism. You must pronounce it Chabalism as if it started with a Spanish hard H – the one that is accompanied by a sound indicating a readiness to spit. Correcting your opponent's pronunciation is worth any number of points.

The Qabalah is a form of mysticism and/or magic which evolved from Judaism and which forms the basis of three-quarters of modern occult thought. In simple terms it covers all the bits of the Old Testament that no-one understands.

It takes many years of earnest study and practise just to master the merest fraction of it. So if you meet anyone at a party under the age of 50 purporting to know anything about it they are probably talking through their hat.

If they start to argue with you and sound as if they might just know something (see key words) then go immediately to plan one. Say "What kind of Qabalism are we talking about here . . . are you talking about pure Jewish Qabalism?" If they say 'Yes' then your sole interest is in the non-Jewish Quabalism that started with Eliphas Levi and the French Magical revival. If they say 'No' you ridicule all non-Jewish Qabalism and insist that it is not worth discussing Qabalism unless it is the original Hebrew kind.

Key words:

Gematria – A very serious business which takes great interest in all the numbers in the Bible and interprets their significance. It is therefore significant that a beast should have seven heads and it would be very bad form to wander in the desert or float in an ark for say 41 days, for instance.

Tetragrammaton – The four letter name of God – *Yod, He, Vau, He* – normally pronounced Jehovah or Yahweh by Christians, but never attempted by Jews who will say Adonai instead. It is said that God created the world by pronouncing the Tetragrammaton correctly and it is regarded as the ultimate magical word of power. As ancient Hebrew does not have any vowels it is anybody's guess how it really is pronounced, but it is suggested that if anyone did say the name correctly the world would end. Please do not experiment as some people have already booked their holidays.

Shekinah – Wisdom, given a female personification. She is mentioned in all the really obscure parts of Proverbs that no-one reads in church. Achieving knowledge is likened to sexual union with Shekinah, which probably explains the rather eccentric meaning of the word to 'know' in the old Testament.

The Tree of Life – The central symbol in Qabalism giving the path to perfection. This is the Tree of Life mentioned in Genesis – not to be confused with the Tree of Knowledge of Good and Evil. The idea is that you follow a complicated path of spiritual enlightenment up the tree passing through each sphere or Sepher until you meet God in Kether the Crown. (Note the plural of Sepher is Sephiroth and not Sephers.) Beyond Kether there is Ain Soph which can be summed up as the Piece of God which passes all understanding.

Knights Templar

The Knights Templar are almost in the Atlantis league with the number of theories that have been thought up about them. Most popular just now are:

a) that they looked after the Shroud of Turin
b) that they guarded the secret knowledge of Rennes-le-Chateau
c) that they were homosexual Satanists
d) that they conspired with the CIA to assassinate President Kennedy.

Admittedly any group of men that would leave home and families to ride off to the Holy Land, just to keep the roads clear for pilgrims must have been a bit strange to begin with.

Romantically minded occultists have always been convinced that the Knights must have had some tremendous secret knowledge that caused them to be persecuted in the way that they were. The more prosaic just accept that the King of France needed money and the easiest way to get it was to accuse the Knights of indulging in bestial rites, burn them at the stake, and keep their vast wealth.

He couldn't do this without a good reason, so he sat up all night thinking up Baphomet, a suitably Eastern sounding idol with the head and feet of a goat, the breasts of a woman and the wings of an angle.

This was a great stroke of luck for occult thriller writers and horror film directors and Baphomet has retained pride of place as the most imaginative image of evil invented. The other great service King Philippe did for modern occultists was that he burnt all the Templars before they could blurt out what their secret really was. This leaves it up for grabs to anyone looking for a pedigree. It also fills in a rather vague bit of history from the 12th to the 14th centuries.

Gnosticism

This was a main competitor to Christianity in Rome when things were just beginning to happen. It was very like Christianity in many ways except for the fact that they couldn't decide whether to spell Jesus' name as Christos or Chrestos which, as all Gematrians and Greek scholars know, makes a world of difference.

It is reckoned that the beliefs of both cults got a little bit mixed up at times so it always safe to assume that anything you don't understand in the New Testament is Gnostic (e.g. anything to do with beasts with seven heads or long discussions about what the word was in the beginning – see Qabalism).

As everyone knows it is not a good idea to be on the losing side in a battle for religious supremacy (see witchcraft). The Gnostics actually came last. They suddenly found themselves adepts of every black art known to man. This is quite ironic as they had previously come up with the theory that the Christian Jehovah was not the real God but an evil creator of an evil world, e.g. the Devil, neatly turning all the Jews and Christians into Devil worshippers.

As it is, the best documented details about them are those written in Christian anti-Gnostic propaganda. This has not stopped people writing long books about what the Gnostics really thought, and it certainly doesn't stop them claiming apostolic succession back to the Gnostics.

If making unlikely comments about the Gnostics always make up a spurious Book of Albert or something that has just been found at the bottom of the pile in the Dead Sea Scrolls. In line with tradition, anything in the Dead Sea Scrolls they don't understand is presumed to be Gnostic.

Key words:

Demiurge – An evil creator who tried to trick everyone into believing he was God while the real God stood in the background being mysterious. The trick was to get past the Demiurge.

Sophia – A female personification of wisdom, like the Qabalists Shekinah, but with strong Greek influence. There was an even stronger sexual connection since she was a prostitute. As such she supposedly knew a thing or two.

Gnosis – Occult buzz-word usually nothing to do with Gnosticism but meant to imply 'I know something that you don't'. It is important never to explain your idea of 'Gnosis' in terms which could possibly be understood.

Cathars – A French sect thought to be the true successors to the Gnostics' Gnosis. No-one really knows because they all got burnt before we could find out.

Rosicrucians

Watch out. There are people calling themselves Rosicrucians who keep putting strange ads in the newspapers. Don't enter discussions about present day Rosicrucianism as there might be one about.

The Order of the Rosy Cross is one of the all-time classic mysterious orders. It was invented as a joke by Johann Valentin Andreae who anonymously published three short books in Germany in the 1610's.

One was *Fama Fratentitas*, the story of Christian Rosenkreuz (the eponymous Rosy Cross) who was supposed to have started a brotherhood of the Rosy Cross in the 15th century. Another tract, *The Chemical Wedding*, was a typical piece of alchemical writing, i.e. it didn't make any sense. The place was buzzing with people wanting to lay their hands on this secret knowledge.

Later Andreae admitted to the world that it was a gigantic leg-pull but due to the fact that mystics are usually pretty limited in their sense of humour, people have been claiming to have this pool of knowledge in direct succession ever since.

This is very useful for bluffers as everyone still hasn't a clue what it was all about. Arthur Waite took nearly 650 pages in his definitive book *The Brotherhood of the Rosy Cross* to come to the conclusion that no-one had a clue what it was all about.

Mystery Religions

Mystery religions were very popular, especially around Rome, because of a clever ruse. Instead of going round the doors trying to sell people *Watch Tower* they suggested that anyone who wanted to join would have to go through years of rigorous training to make them worthy to be accepted. Of course, that had people queuing up to get in.

Best known by far were the Eleusian Mysteries. After years of complicated initiation the final revelation consisted of the seeker after knowledge having an ear of corn pressed into his hand. Perhaps the main mystery therefore was how they kept getting people to join. The mysteries were generally based on fertility cults usually involving the rites of Dionysus who, by all accounts, had almost as much fun as Aleister Crowley.

Alchemy

Alchemy has had a very bad press but it is worthy of any true bluffer's support, if only because it gave occult bluffers their motto. 'Obscurum per obscurius, ignotum per ignotius' is what you would often hear one alchemist say to another over a pint in the evening after a hard day at the Great Work.

What this roughly means is 'Explain obscurity with obscurity, the unknown with the unknown' but it is much more impressive in the Latin, and should only be translated as a last resort.

The alchemists lived up to this by never calling anything by its name but attributing a symbol instead. You end up with a cross between Cockney rhyming slang, and a Jungian analyst having a nervous breakdown.

For instance, a typical Alchemical diary would read 'Took the *Black Bird* from the *Bath* and mixed with the *Red Dragon*. Had to stop because of the appearance of the *Grey Wolf*. Instead entered the *Lion* and the *Unicorn*.' All serious scholars who study alchemy think that the Black Bird is Mercury and the Red Dragon is Sulphur and are searching desperately for the meaning of the other symbols. What they don't know is the Grey Wolf was his Mother-in-Law and the Lion and the Unicorn was the pub he went to, to get away from her.

16

This makes Alchemy ideal for bluffers. All you need to do is adopt any suitable Alchemist symbol for your own purposes. For example, declare: "We take a pint of Guinness – the mysterious *black crow* of the Alchemists – and some bacon – the Alchemical *slaughter of the innocents*, then all we need to make the operation complete is the Philosopher's Egg" and frankly no-one can argue.

To carry this off effectively you have to convince your audience that Alchemists were not deluded persons who gave themselves brain damage heating up mercury to turn scrap metal into gold.

The best suggestion is that the Alchemists weren't really interested in gold at all. They wanted to find the Philosopher's Stone for its ability to purify the soul, and its strange effects on base metals were a mere side issue. Unlikely, but worth a try.

It is also interesting to note that Alchemists thought that metals had genders and new metals were created when two elements joined in sexual union.

Key words:

Squaring the circle – The first step in the Great Work, and the subject of Leonardo da Vinci's famous drawing 'Man with four arms'.

The Serpent Ouroboros – The famous symbol of a snake with its tail in its mouth. The Celts used it to signify eternity, but the Alchemists used it to suggest equilibrium. How any creature can maintain any equilibrium while biting its own bum is not explained.

Philosopher's Stone – That which was said to prolong life indefinitely. Count Cagliostro claimed to be several thousand years old through the effects of the stone. He may still be claiming it.

Egyptians

Egypt is very important to occult thinking – a fact that cannot be put down completely to all those Hammer Horror films about 'The Mummy'. For instance there is always interest in the age old question 'Why did the Egyptian Gods always turn sideways when they were getting their pictures painted?'

Although there are a number of gods to remember, you are usually pretty safe because they changed their names every few centuries and it was virtually impossible most of the time to tell Re-Aten from Amun-Ra, if there ever was a difference.

So if someone mentions, for example, the sun god Ra, always correct that to Ammon-Re. Or vice versa. If they question why, say "Surely by the Middle Kingdom (if you can't remember the kingdom make up a likely sounding one) he was established as Ammon (or Amun)-Ra (or Re). It was only in the Old Kingdom that he was solely Ra (or Re)-Atum (or Aten)." If they then reply with something like "But I was talking about the Thinite period which comprises the First and Second Dynasties and therefore must be before the First Intermediate Period which comprised dynasties seven to ten" immediately say "Right enough. Silly me," and quickly leave the conversation. You have either met an Egyptologist or a master bluffer.

It is a good idea to remember a few of the Egyptian Pantheon as it was the first one, and everyone pinched from it mercilessly. You can therefore look very smart saying things like "Of course Astarte was really just the Canaanite Isis".

There is the classic trinity:

Isis – Mother – Archetype Mother Goddess type. Liked the moon a lot and all that sort of thing.

Osiris – Father – Dying God King figure. Not too bright.

Horus – Little baby – Up and coming type. Difficult to tell who Horus took after as he had the head of a falcon.

Set – The baddy – Brother of Osiris. Instead of wearing a black hat he had jackal's head. Should have made him pretty easy to pick out in a crowd.

The gist of the story is that Set decided to cut his brother up into 15 pieces ("Numerologically that is very significant as it the number of parts in the male body" – Classic Bluffers numerological interruption No. 4) and spread them round the world. Isis then went round trying to find all the bits to put him together again. One can't help feeling that in her grief she was maybe not thinking too logically. She nearly did it, but she could only find 14 pieces – no prizes for guessing which bit was still missing.

This set the scene for Mother Goddesses and Dying God Kings for virtually every religion for the next few thousand years. This made it very popular with occultists in the early part of this century who saw it as the basic symbolism for all religious thinking – apart from those who were busy trying to prove that Qabalism was the basis of all religious thought.

The Egyptophiles were helped by the fact that archaeologists kept dropping like flies from the various curses on Egyptian tombs. This impressed occultists no end. It was reckoned that if Egyptian magic could allow a pharoah to kill a complete stranger after a thousand years it could surely make someone invisible, or something simple, nowadays.

It was also useful that all the gods and goddesss had nice resonant names that sounded good in rituals. Calling on Thoth and Horus was a lot simpler than invoking Sung tzu niang-niang or Bodhisattva Avalo-kitesvara. The robes weren't that hot but you got the chance to wear a lot of eye make-up.

The Hermetic Order of the Golden Dawn were passionate about Egypt and of course Crowley proclaimed the start of the age of Horus the Child and developed a Tarot pack called the Thoth pack full of Egyptian symbolism and notable because the cards are too big to shuffle.

Hermetic Order of the Golden Dawn

It is easy to tell occultists from non-occultists by mentioning the Order of the Golden Dawn. Non-occultist will never have heard of it. A literate non-occultist may know it was the group that Yeats was involved in. The occultist knows it was the group that brought together MacGregor Mathers, Arthur Waite, Aleister Crowley and some Irish poet.

Old occultist's bloodshot eyes light up at the mention of the Golden Dawn. Never before in the history of mankind has such an unlikely bunch of people gathered together to perform such unlikely acts.

It started in a typically obscure way. A coded letter was found in an old book by a Dr Wynn Wescott. He translated it to discover that it was from a Fraulein Anna Sprengel who was running a German version of the Golden Dawn. It is said that if anyone could translate the cypher they could start up their own branch. You can't help feeling that there must be an easier way of launching a membership drive.

Luckily Wescott was just the man to do that, and with a few friends he started the British Order. They gathered together all the occult knowledge they could lay their hands on and tried to turn it into a logical system – a very commendable, if not very practical, idea. They laid out all the knowledge in neat sections with a path of initiation. You had to take examinations to go from grade to grade – a bit like the Boy Scouts, except that women could join and the uniforms were more impressive.

They opened a lovely temple in London and then branched out by opening others in Edinburgh, Paris and Bradford (a hot-bed of occult activity). They produced masses of really impressive sounding ceremonies. They all thought up fancy new names for themselves like Fra Semper Vigilante or Fra Lux E Tenebris. And then they all fell out with each other.

Some of the group (most notably Waite) wanted to go into new and even more exciting forms of mysticism while another group (including MacGregor Mathers and Crowley) wanted to go further into magic. It didn't help that Mathers was going mad and Crowley was already there waiting for him.

Key words:

Grades – A system under which you started as a Neophyte and worked your way through to Magus, when you discovered that MacGregor Mathers had discovered another order and you still had another 43 grades to go through.

Hermetic – To do with Hermes, the Greek God of Magic and the inventor of the air-tight seal.

MAGIC

There are a number of different types of magic which it is always worth knowing. Details are usually found in books called grimoires. In films these are massive tomes, three feet thick, bound in leather. In reality they are normally pathetically thin, padded out with four thousand line drawings of pentacles and Hebrew words.

The important thing when writing grimoires was to include a list of items vitally necessary to complete the exercise. You then made sure that there were at least two items which are impossible to obtain – maybe the compassion of a traffic warden or the sincerity of a politician. Of course it is not like making a curry where if you don't have chilli powder you just bung in a spoonful of curry powder and hope for the best.

Thus, when an irate customer complained about a totally ineffective potion for whipping up storms, you could say something like "Did you use a left or right eye of a newt?" or "Are you certain that cat was completely black?"

Sympathetic Magic

Nothing to do with what wonders a cup of tea and a shoulder to cry on can do. The basis of sympathetic or imitative magic is that there is a connection between an object and a symbol.

For example, you make up a doll to look like someone you don't like, stick a thorn in it and bingo – the person in question gets stabbing pains in his back. Or get some hair or nail clippings and burn them and the victim gets a fever.

It's not always to do something unpleasant. The best

way to make sure that you have a bumper harvest is to carry out the procreative act in the furrows after ploughing your field.

Key words:

Mandrake – The best example of a sympathetic magic substance. A rather mysterious plant that was supposed to do everything, but whose main use seems to have been as an aphrodisiac due to its shape which was taken to resemble a part of the male anantomy. You couldn't harvest Mandrake in the normal way as the scream it gave as it left the ground would kill you or drive you mad. Instead you tied it to a dog's collar, went out of earshot and whistled the dog. How the dog is supposed to hear you if you're out of earshot is your problem.

Shamanism

This is a type of mysticism and magic associated with the Shamans or witch-doctors of the North American Indians. It is an ecstatic form of magic usually involving dancing a lot, drinking strange colourless liquids and smoking strange-smelling substances. You really get the feeling they enjoy their work.

The Shamans, after several hours of this effort, go into a little hut all alone and perform miraculous and totally inexplicable acts. For instance, they can miraculously travel long distances. So instead of sitting at Heathrow waiting for the traffic controllers' strike to end you can go into a small room, dance, drink and smoke, and end up in Ibiza. The power of this has been proven recently, strangely enough, in reverse. It seems people have gone to Ibiza, drunk, smoked and danced a lot and ended up in a small room.

But their powers do not stop here. As well as being able to transport themselves over vast distances they always managed to get back again to the same little hut they left. Amazing really.

They are also supposed to do terribly serious, difficult things like curing ill people and appeasing the gods, but quite frankly would you bother if you could just pop over to Ibiza instead?

The best thing about Shamanism is that if it doesn't work it's not your fault as you were in an ecstatic state and weren't in control of your faculties. The fact that you were out of your skull on sangria in a disco in Ibiza is incidental. And it always gives you an excuse for dancing, smoking and drinking all over again the next night.

Ritual Magic

Ritual or ceremonial magic depends on things sounding and looking good. It involves dressing up in fancy robes and proclaiming impressive sounding names in Egyptian, Latin or Hebrew. English words can only be used if they're really archaic or really long.

One essential belief is that if you know the real name of something you have some control over it. Get to know the real name of a demon for instance and you're laughing. However, there is a flaw. Demon's names will virtually always be given in ancient Hebrew where you are given the consonants and have to guess at the vowels. You can while away many long winter nights standing in a draughty pentacle trying every conceivable permutation of a five syllable demon's name.

It is also important to get every detail of the ceremony right. Say one word wrong or point your ceremonial sword to the wrong point of the compass and you've blown the whole thing.

This is a very British form of magic as it doesn't involve pounding drums or mixing things – just an accountant's attention to detail and the ability to look good in a silk night-gown.

Key words:

Words of Power – Words that release a special power just by saying them or writing them on the correct amulet. Abracadabra is a word of power mentioned in the famous grimoire, *The Key Of Solomon The King*.

Names of Power – Mainly different names for God or the Angels. Ritual magic grimoires usually read like a Hebrew telephone directory. Even more useful would be the real names of the demons, but these all seem to be ex-directory.

Abra-Melin

Abra-Melin is the most commonly claimed form of magical exercise. In line with occultists' ideas for snappy titles, the book in which this knowledge is contained is called *The book of the Sacred Magic of Abra-Melin, the Mage, as delivered by Abraham the Jew unto his Son Lamach*. It was translated into English (or a close approximation) by MacGregor Mathers.

The idea of Abra-Melin is that man holds the middle ground between the angels and the fallen angels (i.e. demons) and that he can perform feats of magic by gaining control over these demons with the help of the angels. To make it slightly more difficult, these demons are wily little rascals that will trick you into doing what they want to do (thus explaining why Satanism is a bad idea). The only way to make sure you don't get tricked is to go into a long process of purification of the soul to get rid of all the base desires and petty hopes of gain.

Unfortunately having got rid of all these base desires you need a good imagination to work out why you need your new-found magical powers. This is particularly useful to bluffers as you can claim to have completed the operation but still refuse to prove the fact because you have got rid of all petty desires to show off.

As always there are a number of safety valves to ensure that no-one is stupid enough to seriously try out Abra-Melin magic.

1. You have to buy a house in a secluded place with windows all round and a terrace covered completely to a depth of two fingers with pure river sand. Go in to any estate agents and ask for that des res and see what choice you have.

2. You then have to tell your servant you are not taking calls for six months and set to work on the programme of exercises. If you are carrying out the operation to get your hands on some money you could be facing some problems.

3. Then the clincher. For six months you must not eat animal flesh, drink alcohol and must constantly think about spiritual matters. That should put everyone off.

Key words:

Oratory – The room of your residence where you have to eat vegetables and think good thoughts.

Invoke – What you do to the Angels.

26

Conjure – What you do the Evil Spirits.

NB: Do not try to Invoke Evil Spirits or Conjure Angels as this can cause confusion.

Witchcraft

Witchcraft is in effect the old Druidic Mother Goddess religion in Britain. It was a competitor with Christianity and as everyone knows it is not a good idea to lose a religious battle for supremacy. Wicca or Witchcraft didn't even get second place.

Being a Mother Goddess religion the priests of the religion were of course, women – 'wise' women. These proved very handy for dropping into water to see if they would float, and burning; the sort of activity that gives the whole village a day out and keeps their minds off the fact that the price of a pint of beer has just rocketed to a farthing.

To underline just how evil these poor old women were, the Church neatly redefined their idea of the Devil. There is a precedent for this, it happens with monotonous regularity in the Bible.

What they did was to turn any male deities into a personification of the Devil. So if you worshipped Herne the Hunter ergo you became a Devil worshipper and should be dunked in water and/or burnt. If it happened that the local tribe had a goat as their totem animal that immediately became a symbol of evil. You can understand why goats were confused.

Everyone who knew anything about witchcraft was either dropped in a river or burnt a long while ago so modern day witchcraft is usually made up as it goes along.

Key words:

Widdershins – The way you can tell if you have come up against a really evil bunch of Black witches or Devil worshippers: when they dance in a circle, they go widdershins – anti-clockwise. You can't help feeling there must be more to it than that.

Coven – A bunch of people that like to get together every so often, take all their clothes off and dance about . . . in the open air.

Ley-lines – What they call the queues at all the orgies they're supposed to have.

Witch-trials – A bit like sheep dog trials but a lot more fun.

Sexual Magic

Say "sexual magic" and everyone immediately thinks of Aleister Crowley: he did so much to make the subject very much his own. In fact, he was only following up a line of succession that has run through magic and mysticism for thousands of years.

The idea behind it is that at the moment of sexual climax you release a power than can be tapped for magical ends.

People like Crowley went a step or two further (in Crowley's case 15 or 16 steps further) by indulging in every depravity they could think of and introducing a suggestion box to get a few more ideas. This allowed them to reach a state of sexual exhaustion in which they could achieve the ecstatic and magically potent state of mystics. As the mystics usually had to fast for a few months and then flog themselves for a couple of weeks more to get to the same state, Crowley and friends reckoned they were going the sensible way about it.

Crowley was not the only one to indulge in sexual magic. He got the idea from the Ordo Templis Orientis, a German organisation complete with regulation cyphers and Secret Chiefs. You can't help feeling that the story-line owes a little to the Golden Dawn and Anna Sprengler.

Another branch of sexual magic was performed by Frenchman Joseph-Antoine Boullan who taught that you could improve yourself only by having sexual intercourse with arch angels, saints and historical figures. On the other end of the scale he said that you could help animals come up the evolutionary scale by the same method, but we won't go into that. He performed ceremonies called *The Sacrifice of Glory of Melchizedek* and *The Privictimal Sacrifice of Mary* with his priestess – a spectacle very popular with visitors to his Church of Carmel, seemingly.

There certainly was a strong sexual element in Gnosticism (those agape suppers weren't all platonic love it seems) and there were times when copulation was needed in Qabalism (although strictly between husband and wife so as not to offend the Jewish sense of morality). You can't say it was a part of the old fertility cults. It was all there was in them. Devotees would not turn up to religious ceremonies without an orgy or a bit of religious prostitution.

Modern day witches make loud noises about how straight-laced their ceremonies are, although some admit that they are not the sort of thing you would take you maiden aunt to – just in case she enjoyed it.

Black Magic/White Magic

The idea of Black and White Magic comes about through a particularly British notion that magic is like electricity – sitting about in the plug waiting to be used. You can use it to warm an electric blanket or to electrocute someone. In the same way magic doesn't mind how it's used.

Naturally everyone who admits to being involved in magic is only interested in White Magic. Even out-of-the-closet Satanist spend hours proving that they are not really bad – just misunderstood.

The only problem with this is that there are a very limited amount of things that you can do with White Magic, and the vast majority of them have been taken over by the National Health Service.

Witches get involved in rather mundane things like ceremonies to ensure that the sun rises every morning and that summer returns after winter but you can't help feeling that they are not getting any real job satisfaction.

On the other hand Black Magicians won't admit that they are using magic to do what everyone would want to use it for – to gain money, power and sex.

This is what makes magic so difficult to quantify. The ones that admit to doing it are only doing things that no-one is interested in, and you don't know if those not admitting to it are getting the results or not.

Still that has to be the fun of magic. If you did happen to find the totally black cat and said the words just right and pointed your ceremonial sword in exactly the right direction, maybe you might just raise a storm or make yourself invisible.

Mysticism

An interest in mysticism is vital for any quality bluffer. For a start there are only 12 people in the world that know what the word means and you would have to be pretty unlucky to meet one of them at a party. In fact people's lack of knowledge is so profound that they cannot even formulate a sensible question about it, so you don't even need to learn any key words. Someone might just ask you a technical question about the path from Malkuth to Daath in the Qabalah but what are they going to ask you about mysticism? This means that you can appear to be an expert on what is presumably a vast, immensely deep subject without having to do anything.

It is also invaluable as an escape route for getting out of tight corners. This is due to the fact that there are not even 12 people in the world that *want* to know what mysticism is.

Therefore when you are being pushed for some solid facts, say on Alchemy, you just point out that your interest in the subject is "purely mystical." At that point you just watch your opponent's eyes glaze over and you know the battle is won.

It also means that you do not have to prove any magical powers in a concrete way. An interest in mysticism means that you use all the powers you gain only to working towards achieving union with the God-head. So just drop into any conversation that you really enjoyed last Friday evening because you achieved union with the God-head and no-one can argue.

Finally and most importantly, no-one will believe you. It is reckoned that anyone who would waste as much time as you obviously have, gaining such a vast accumulation of secret lore must be doing it for a reason. By telling them you are not doing it for any personal gain you will force them to immediately disbelieve you and therefore you leave them to use their imagination as to why you are doing it. And as everyone knows, the powers of imagination are even more powerful than the powers of magic.

THE BLACK ARTS

You cannot claim a comprehensive knowledge of the occult without a look at the darker side. So here is a round-up of the real black arts.

Satanism

The development of Satanism is a perfect example of the powers of propaganda and public relations. Christianity comes to Britain and one of the early Church fathers has the bright idea of telling everyone that the old fertility religion that they used to follow is actually worshipping the Devil. (See Witchcraft and Gnosticism.)

They convince everyone that the local god is the Devil in disguise and then put it about that his worshippers cavort about in the nude, indulge in abandoned group sex and drink heavily. Then they wonder why they are losing even more people from their flock.

The Church Fathers scratch their heads a bit and come up with the idea of telling everyone that these devil worshippers eat children, sacrifice virgins, drink urine and defile graves. This works for most of the congregation but of course there has to be one person who thinks "That sounds like fun too really. I'll need to give it a try next full moon." And so Satanism is born.

The essence of it is that you should act in the most bestial and offensive fashion you can think of – like some sort of mystical Hell's Angel – and you will attract the attention of the infernal being and he will reward you with super-human powers. That's the theory, anyway.

Whether anyone has ever got any super-human

powers is debatable, but by the time the Satanists have finished:
a) turning crosses upside down
b) using a prostitute's naked body as an altar
c) drinking and eating all sort of unmentionable things instead of the host;
they have got so used to their depravities, they keep doing it just for the fun.

Key words:

Black Mass – Supposedly a serious Satanic ceremony, although it seems more popular as a particularly lurid night club act.

Key phrases:

'Do unto others as they do unto you' – The motto of the Church of Satan*. You wonder how many long winter nights they sat up thinking up that one.

Voodoo

We have chosen Voodoo to represent all the ethnic magics typified by witch-doctors with bones round their necks that exist everywhere in the world. Voodoo is quite interesting in that it contains elements of Shamanism, sympathetic magic and even some ritual magic.

It also has one unique element worth considering – zombies. These are dead people who have been raised from their graves to work as mindless slaves for powerful Voodoo exponents. It was popularly thought

* There is now an offical Church of Satan in San Francisco. It is not affiliated to the World Council of Churches.

that this magic didn't work on white men until recent tests proved that three-quarters of the travellers on British Rail commuter trains on a Monday morning are in fact zombies.

Creatures of the Night

You may feel that creatures of the night need not worry the occultist of today. With your medallion against the evil eye and your amulet and pentacle for protection against astral attack, why should you worry?

Unfortunately people seem totally obsessed by them. Although it is inadvisable to get into the habit of telling gruesome tales of ghastly ghouls it is worthwhile having a few words that can be dragged out of you on the subject.

Vampires
Even before the days of Hammer Horror films occultists took vampires seriously. These creatures didn't physically drink blood but it was thought that some people could stay young by drawing the life and vitality from the people round them leaving them broken, worn out shells. They are still about today, only we call them toddlers.

Werewolves
The word to use when discussing Werewolves is 'shape-shifting'. They don't turn into a wolf at the full moon, they shift their shape. There are all sorts of were creatures (were means man, by the way) so you can get werebears, werejaguars, weregerbils – whatever you fancy.

By a strange coincidence, stories of werewolves died

out about the same time as rabies in this country. Another influence was the memory of the famous Nordic 'berserkers' who ate wolf flesh and dressed in wolf skins to take on the attributes of their totem animal (sympathetic magic). Anyone who would bite the edge off his shield because he couldn't wait to get into battle had to make an impression.

The theory that they could only be killed by a silver bullet was started by the press office of the Guild of Silversmiths.

Incubi/Succubi

These impressively named creatures of the night are evil spirits that visit people by night to tempt them with all manner of lusts and depravities. They choose someone of pure character and appear to them in the shape of an attractive person of the opposite sex. After these nasty creatures have had their evil way, the victim is left feeling drained and weak.

Any husband using the excuse today will have to come up with a good reason why the Succubus happened to take the shape of the barmaid at the Pig and Feathers. Not advised nowadays, but you have to admit that the person that thought it up first must have been an all-time master bluffer.

FAMOUS NAMES

It is always useful having a good name to drop and the names below are reasonably good all-rounders. Please note that they all are dead, some for quite a while, so if you do insist on mentioning that you spoke to them last week, have a convincing story about a seance or automatic writing to back it up.

All are given are obscurity ratings out of 10. The names with low obscurity ratings you need to know most details about as they are well known, but never quote them as someone might just know enough to argue. The high obscurity ratings are those that virtually no-one knows about unless they check up afterwards. To learn the details is optional and you can quote them freely on their pet subjects.

Dr John Dee (1527 – 1608)

Dr John must go down in history as the most gullible man to walk the face of the earth. He managed to get in tow with a certain Edward Kelly who persuaded the good doctor that he could communicate with angels. This they did in a very long and complicated process which involved Kelly pointing to letters or shouting them in reverse order (all the words were backwards for some reason never fully explained) while the doctor wrote them down. The process was made slightly more difficult by the fact that the words thus spelt were all in Enochian, that well known language of the angels. This proves once and for all it is not Gaelic.

The result is the book *A True and Faithful Relation of what passed between Doctor John Dee and some spirits* – a snappy title which guaranteed it a spectacular commerical success. The first edition came out in 1659 followed up almost immediately by a limited edition printed in 1974. This is naturally a classic of occult literature and was a great influence on the Order of the Golden Dawn, and of course, Crowley. (At that time even the 1974 edition had not been published so it was really safe to be an expert on it.)

There were also one or two actual spirits who appeared to the pair including Madimi a spirit in the shape of a eight year old child. Dee eventually did become a little suspicious when Kelly informed him that Madimi had stated that they should have all things in common, including their wives. The successful partnership broke up just after that, seemingly at the instigation of Mrs Dee.

Key words:

Skrying – Dee's particularly obscure form of talking to the angels. It involved moving a skrying stone (a crystal ball) on a tablet covered with Enochian letters. Fortunately it is not that important as no-one else has been stupid enough to use the same method for several hundred years.

Enochian – The language of the angels complete with its own grammar and syntax and about as easy to understand as dialect Serbo-Croat. Luckily the angels seemed to take a crash course in English or Hebrew just after this.

Pet subjects – Enochian and crystal gazing.
Obscurity level 10/10.

Eliphas Levi (1810 – 1875)
Old Eliphas was the father of all the modern occultists. He started several traditions:

a) He was the first to adopt an impressive name. He was originally Alphonse Louis Constant which he translated into dog Hebrew as Eliphas Levi Zahed.

He dropped the Zahed as it put him too near the end of the telephone directory.

b) He was one of the first with a penchant for being photographed in ceremonial robes looking grand and slightly sinister. This was not quite as impressive a piece of originality as you might think for he had the luck to be around just as the camera was being invented.

c) He had a most impressive beard which helped him no end.

d) He was a failed Catholic priest (well nearly – he didn't quite take orders) a very popular background for occultists.

e) He made a perilous living teaching occultism and wrote countless books on the Qabalah and Magic.

f) He cleverly refused to perform any magical acts as he regarded them extremely dangerous both morally and physically (bluffers' rule No 4.)

The only time he was stupid enough to attempt anything practical was when he tried a touch of Necromancy to raise the spirit of Appolonius of Tyana. Appolonius was a rather vague Pythagorean occultist of the first century of whom a great number of stories had been made up to the extent that no-one is really sure if he ever existed. Why Levi couldn't have stuck to a Red Indian spirit guide or a 'recently passed over dear one' has never been explained.

The result was a dismal failure. Appolonius appeared (which would seem to suggest that he had existed), took exception to Levi pointing a sword at him, touched him on the arm and Levi fainted. This did not stop the great man dining out on the story for many years and writing the classic *The Dogma and Ritual of Transcendental Magic*. You can't help wondering what he would have done if he had forced even one word out of the old ghost.

Special interests – Qabalism and the Tarot.
Obscurity rating 8/10.

Blavatsky (1831 – 1891)

Mme Helena Petrovna Blavatsky was the founder of Theosophy – God knows why she called it that. No-one knows about her early days so it is not certain that she made up the name, but it seems too good to be true. So does the story that she was an exiled Russian aristocrat.

After the normal sort of apprenticeship for a religious leader (medium and snake charmer) she founded Theosophy. The main aim of the movement was to spread knowledge of Eastern mysticism to such an extent that she virtually single-handedly introduced and made known all those vague philosophies and religions that are so popular now. So next time you are pestered in the street by someone with a shaven head in saffron long-johns you know who to blame.

At first sight Theosophy seems an ideal movement to claim as a link in your chain of occult knowledge. It has the rather obscure mystical content that would normally be perfect, and even Secret Chiefs. But be warned. There are still Theosophists about and it would be just your luck to meet one.

Instead you should have a reasonable working knowledge of the historical perspective (when someone mentions "Blavatsky" don't say "Who's he?") but discount modern day Theosophy totally.

Blavatsky had a strong influence on the British magical revival and numbered Arthur Waite amongst her flock until they fell out. He just didn't seem to get on with anyone. She wrote a large number of thick books *(Isis Unveiled, The Secret Doctrine)* packed full of detail à la *Golden Bough* interspersed with very complicated creation mythologies which don't really improve much on the Genesis one, but certainly took up more space.

She also discredited the business of Secret Masters which must have been very upsetting for the leaders of a number of vague occult groups who depended on the aid of Secret Masters to get unpopular decisions carried out. Well, it must be difficult to differentiate between letters from Mahatmas that have just materialised, and letters that an accomplice has pushed through a hole in the ceiling.

Key words:

Hidden Chiefs or Mahatmas – Blavatsky's mystical pen pals: a nice bunch of adepts from Tibet who used to make letters to her materialise round the house in the oddest little corners. Absolutely nothing to do with people crawling through the attic and dropping letters through cracks in the ceiling. Honest.

Astral Light – Something like a personal anglepoise but cheaper to run.

MacGregor-Mathers (1854 – 1917)

Samuel Liddell Mathers was actually a Scot so he probably had as much right to claim to be a Highland chieftain as any of the modern occultists, although suddenly discovering the title le Comte de Glenstrae was thought a little extravagant. If he had stuck to his first assumed name, MacGregor Mathers, probably no-one would have noticed.

He was one of the founders of the Hermetic Order of the Golden Dawn and by far the most interesting. He ended up in France having long chats with Hidden and/or Secret Chiefs whom only he could talk to, and becoming gradually more and more obsessed by Black

Magic. As well as finding a title he didn't know he had, he discovered a Third Order of a level of initiation that no-one else seemed to know about.

This didn't go down with the run of the mill Golden Dawners who threw him out of the order. At this Mathers sent Crowley from France in full Highland costume with a golden dagger at his side to snatch back the Temple. The Golden Dawners said 'Go away' and Crowley decided to take them to court instead. Don't ask why he didn't use magic. Mathers then fell out with Crowley too. You can't help feeling a copy of *How to Win Friends and Influence People* would have been invaluable in these circles.

Interests – Ritual/Black Magic and talking to Secret Chiefs.
Obscurity rating 8/10.

Stanilas de Guaita (1871 – 1898)

De Guaita was by far the most fun of French occultists that followed Levi. He is best known for having an astral battle with a certain Joseph-Antoine Boullan, a defrocked priest who came up with the perfectly reasonable theory that you approached God by having sexual intercourse with celestial beings.

De Guaita and another occultist Oswald Wirth decided to expose Boullan as a fraud and wrote him a letter saying that he was a condemned man. Boullan took this as an astral threat and immediately took steps to protect himself.

Despite all his efforts Boullan died under mysterious circumstances just six years later, absolute proof that the spells can sometimes take a long time to work. During this time there were stories of 'fluidic fisticuffs', blasts of cold air that slapped Boullan round the ear and frightened the cat, and it is regarded as the most exciting astral battle ever. De Guaita died at 27 from a drugs overdose, a very suitable end for an occultist.

Specialities – Rosicrucianism, Black Magic and fluidic fisticuffs.
Obscurity rating 9/10.

Arthur Waite (1857 – 1940)
Arthur Waite is worth quoting for three reasons.

1. He was a scholar who actually would give references and reasons for his ideas.
2. He wrote on every occult subject you could wish to mention, and some you wouldn't.
3. His books are so long and crashingly boring that virtually no-one has read them.

His greatest claim to fame is thought to be that he led the mystical clique in the Order of the Golden Dawn at the time it was breaking up and came into conflict with Aleister Crowley. But, since everyone came into conflict with Aleister Crowley, don't play that up too much. Waite also fell out with Helena Blavastsky and the Theosophists so perhaps he wasn't the easiest person to get on with.

He ended up rewriting all the Golden Dawn rituals to tie in with Christian mysticism by which time no-one was interested in the Golden Dawn any more.

His real claim to fame though is that he was the only one of the 19th century mystical thinkers who actually showed any kind of cynicism towards what he was hearing, which probably explains why he fell out with everyone.

Pet subjects – Mysticism, Kabbalah, Tarot, Rosicrucianism and Free Masonry.
Obscurity rating 7/10.

Aleister Crowley (1875 – 1947)

Crowley was dubbed by the *Daily Express* 'The wick-edest man who ever lived' and he spent the whole of his life trying to live up to the title.

He packed a lot of occult action into that time. He is the archetype black-magician used as the model for the bad person in any number of books (for example Somerset Maugham's *The Magician* and every villain in the Dennis Wheatley books.)

He was, for a short time, a member of the Hermetic Order of the Golden Dawn where he managed to fall out with virtually everyone and was involved in the great split.

More in his line was his interest in the OTO (Ordo Templis Orientis), a German order involved in sexual magic, complete with Secret Masters. He took this and adapted it into a new religion, Thelema. With an unac-customed zeal for economy he boiled down the 10 commandments into one – 'Do what thou wilt shall be the whole of the law', a code that on the face of it seems pretty easy to comply with.

Crowley claimed to have completed every magical exercise anyone has ever invented and raised every demon ever heard of and a few he made up himself. It is suggested that when he raised Choronzon, the demon of chaos, he made a mistake by staying outside the pentacle (the only time he used this method) and ended up possessed by this particularly nasty spirit. Or to put it in layman's terms, he was a loony.

Not only did he use the old trick of claiming knowl-edge passed on from every sect or cult known to man Crowley took this a step further by claiming to be a re-incarnation of everyone that he admired in occult history. Just before that particular incarnation he was Eliphas Levi, the French occultist. Unfortunately the great man never mentioned that he was going to be

Aleister Crowley in his next incarnation so the claim
was difficult to verify.

Other claims to fame were that he was the first man
to discover the method for curing cocaine addiction by
getting hooked on heroin and vice versa and that he
worked for the German propaganda service in America
during the First World War. Because of this total
hedonism, giving in to any and every temptation of
the flesh he could think of (and taking a few sugges-
tions from friends) he died tragically young at the age
of 72.

Key words:

Thelema – Crowley's new religion which can be crys-
  tallised in the idea that if you didn't interfere with
  Crowley enjoying himself then you would be all
  right.

Autohagiography – Crowley's version of autobi-
  ography. Even remembering the word is regarded as
  significant. Also never quote a Crowley book by its
  title but as *Liber* and any Roman number you want.
  This avoids being too specific about details. You can
  quote him any any subject. He wrote on the lot.

666 – The Mark of Beast as mentioned in the Book of
  Revelation and adopted by Crowley as his own
  special lucky number.

The Scarlet Woman – Whatever women he was
  involved with at the time, Crowley tried to turn into
  his idea of the Scarlet Woman, a particularly wanton
  prostitute. Most of his abandoned Scarlet Women
  committed suicide or went mad. He was also quite
  keen on men, and his former boyfriends usually
  committed suicide or went mad too.

Pet subjects – Crowley, Magic, Qabalism, Tarot, Sex
and of course, Crowley.
Obscurity level 3/10.

The Devil

You have to be careful if you drop this name in conversation as by all accounts he is still about. It is difficult to tell when you meet him as he goes under several names – the Devil, Old Nick, Satan, Beelzebub, Baphomet, Mephistopheles, Lord of the Flies, etc. You sometimes wonder if he is an embodiment of evil or an entry in *Roget's Thesaurus*.

The reason for the vast range of names is that he has had to incorporate a large number of different personalities. (That, and a desire to avoid the bailiffs.)

Interests – Collecting souls and telling lies.
Ambition – To think up an eighth deadly sin.
Obscurity rating 0/10.

OCCULT SCIENCES

If you are really going to impress people with your esoteric powers you have to do something to prove that you really have powers. At this the casual bluffer begins to get nervous. 'What do you mean, prove?' he asks in a quavering voice.

The seasoned bluffer smiles casually. He knows that it is the easiest thing in the world to prove something to someone who wants to believe. People want magic to exist so they will go to a lot of trouble and ignore the facts to have it proved to them. Those that don't, you just dismiss as eternal sceptics. 'It's amazing how some people will just not accept the facts merely because it upsets their ideas of an established order of things' you say, sadly shaking your head, and those who want it proved will agree whole-heartedly.

The easiest sciences to use as proof are the powers of augury – that's fortune telling but somehow augury sounds better. There are many ways of exploiting precognition (that's fortune telling again) but at the end of the day they all use the same technique of interpretation.

Many of the methods (astrology, palmistry, numerology, phrenology) require that you give a short character study to show how their stars/palm/numbers/ bumps accurately reveal their true personality. If you do this right they will be so pleased they won't listen too closely to your predictions.

Be vague but pleasant – "I can see you have a warm caring personality but you are not a person whose heart rules their head." Give them one or two compliments that sound like faults – "I can see you are not someone who suffers fools glady" or "I see your major failing is that you just can't relax – always have to be doing something."

Be sure to give a vast amount of rather inconsequential detail mentioning travel, problems in their job, arguments at home and a pleasant surprise. There has to be a lot so that they have forgotten most of it by the time they leave. Then when something comes up involving travel, problems at work, etc. they can remember you said something about it, and presume you have predicted it. Always tell them what they want to hear unless it is statistically unlikely. For instance, 'Will I find the man of my dreams before I'm 40?' Answer "Yes": 'Will I win the pools next week?' Answer "No".

Then sit back and take the praise about how accurate your augury is.

Numerology

Numerology is the belief that numbers have an important influence on our lives. It is based on Gematria (see Qabalism) but it has been turned by the profane into a mere parlour trick used only to impress the ignorant. It is therefore invaluable to bluffers. However if you are not good at sums you can get away with ridiculing the whole idea.

Like Gematria it involves turning the letters of names into numbers but while Gematria deals with the names of God, arch-angels and the Sephiroth, Numerology is mainly used for people's names. This is why it is popular and no-one has heard of Qabalism. You mention at a party that you can tell people their characters by the numbers in their name and they queue up with awed wonder written on their faces. Try the same trick with an arch-angel and see how far you get.

You can convert the letters using one of several

systems. That is not important. The important part is manipulating the numbers to suit your ends. Manipulating the numbers is the essence of good bluffing (in fact its the essence of real numerology) and depends on you using some pretty complicated formulae. But it's not as bad as it sounds. You make them up as you go along and don't really need to remember them again.

So when you say "Take away 235 the sacred number of the Incas" you don't actually have to remember the number 235 again. The sacred number of the Incas could be 412 the next time if it suits better.

The simplest system is just to write numbers from 1 to 9 along the top of a piece of paper and then write the letters of the alphabet underneath with A as 1 B as 2 and so on. When you get to J you start at 1 again. Then you read the letters off and choose the relevant number. Add the numbers together and see if you think that number looks significant. If it doesn't add the digits of the number together to get a single number. That has to be significant.

If possible don't let them see you do this. If people see how easy it is they will probably set up as numerologists themselves. If you get to the stage where people look as if they might twig what you're doing switch to another system of numerology.

This is no problem as there are as many numerological systems as there are people writing books on the subject. Most good bluffers just switch between the Pythagorean Music of the Spheres system and the Qabalistic system depending on the IQ of the audience. You can throw in a gratuitous "Of course you know the real number of the mystic pi" as long as you are sure he or she hasn't passed O level Arithmetic.

If you can, use the Qabalistic method as this is, by far, the most impressive. It does involve you in translating people's names into ancient Hebrew so just make sure you don't do it in front of anyone with the vaguest idea of that language. All the charts for this are laid out in *Liber 777* ('The Qabalah of Aleister Crowley' really, but Liber 777 sounds better). Unless you are very brave don't read it, but it does look impressive lying round the coffee table.

Don't be worried about people actually checking up on your arithmetic. Unless you are in a room full of Maths graduates the chances of anyone wanting to check it, far less being able, are very limited. And at the end of the day you can use the old "I'm using the Hebrew method of counting – they count backwards you know" routine.

As well as the name you can take other significant numbers into account. Date of birth, street number, telephone number, number of legs – anything you think you can get away with. You want as many numbers as possible so that if someone says 'You say I'm dependable and boring but really I'm a wild free spirit' then you can say "Well according to your name you are boring and dependable but your birth date added to the number of heads you have come to three" etc, etc.

You can even go on to suggest that they change their name to suit their other numbers. You can say something like "Now if you change your name to Emily that will underline the mystical qualities in your nature" and if he's not keen well that's his hard luck.

People actually did change their names to suit their numbers. The best known example is Aleister Crowley who was christened Alexander. Some unkind people have suggested it was just because he couldn't spell Alexander. He certainly couldn't spell Alasdair.

Another famous example is the Persian god Mithra whose name held the mystical secret of the fact that there are 364 days in the year. When it was discovered that there were in fact 365 days in the year he quickly changed his name to Mithras. And don't forget Abraham (née Abram).

The main thing to remember about numerology is that it makes all numbers significant. So whenever you hear a number being quoted you can say "Now that is significant" and go on to explain that the number 2445 is actually 10 times the mystical pi minus the secret number of Isis plus the outward number of Osiris risen. Then look round smugly, daring anyone to challenge you.

Here are a few key numbers and some words of explanation – more than enough to keep a good bluffer going for a week.

Key numbers:

1 The male principle, warm, creative – A right pain in the neck.

2 The female principle, intuitive, motherly – Trust them as far as you can throw them.

3 Lively, artistic – Talk a lot.

4 Four square, solid, earthy, practical – Incredibly boring.

5 The five senses, ergo sensuality and sex (it had to get in somehow).

6 Romantic, warm, loving – Keep well clear.

7 Mystical – Pretty weird in fact.

8 The number of fate – Unlucky for some.

9 Pretty pushy – Don't pick a fight.

12 Number needed for a coven (except for Satanists who always have 13).

13 – Regarded as unlucky because if you were the 13th you couldn't get into the coven (unless you were a Satanist). Also associated with Judas (13th disciple – not lucky) and the Tarot card Death (still not lucky). However everyone knows this so always point out that in numerology it is not an evil number but signifies a new start in the old duo-decimal system. That should keep them guessing.

40 – The number of days and nights people always did things for in the Bible, either floating about in an ark or wandering in the desert. It is the number of purification. Note that it is always 40 days and 40 nights – not like package holidays: 14 days 12 nights.

666 – The Mark of the Beast. The number of the anti-Christ as made famous in Revelation at the end of the Bible. The only significant number known by occult thriller writers and horror film makers, so therefore generally known to the public. Don't use it.

888 – The Man of Sorrows. The number of associated with Jesus. Not in the Bible so you can use it in a condescending manner if anyone tries to look clever by mentioning 666.

Key phrase:

The language of numbers – It is perfectly possible to claim that occult information has been given to you through the 'language of numbers'. This is usually done through measuring an old building and finding that the number 47 occurs 12 times in the measurements of a tiled floor. You then write a book with all this information and use your undoubted mathematical skills to count your money.

Conversations with the Beyond

An essential part of the esoteric arts is communicating with the dead. This is something that occultists have been interested in since the beginning of time, so you really have to make an attempt.

Spiritualism

This was great fun at the turn of the century, packed full of interesting trumpet blowing and table-shifting. It now seems to have been taken over completely by little old ladies with blue rinses trying to 'Make contact with a loved one recently departed' (which makes you think that the terminology was written by an undertaker who worked for British Rail).

The practical result of this is that admitting to going to a seance is like admitting to going to the Bingo.

Even if you do go, all you hear is 'Yes, Mabel. Your Albert is very happy on the other side' (and looking at Mabel's face you can understand why). No-one asks probing questions like 'How come every spirit guide is a Red Indian? Are there nothing but Red Indians on the other side?'

Ouija

Even the old ouija board has lost its romance by being too accessible. Never regale the company with exciting tales of what happened the night you got the ouija board out. There will always be someone who can top your story with tales of blood pouring out of the tap and ghostly fingers touching his or her face while 'playing' with the ouija.

It could just be possible to get away with it if you

had a great big ouija board that you could stand on and you spelt out the words backwards in Enochian (see Dr Dee) but that's pretty hackneyed now.

The only method left is by far the most dangerous.

Necromancy

Like spiritualism, it's really just talking to the dead, but you must admit Necromancy sounds better. Of course the good bluffer doesn't actually attempt necromancy: that's far too hazardous. The best idea is to talk (or better still just hint) that you have indulged in the awful art.

The real thing involves the usual standing about in draughty pentacles, pointing ceremonial swords at different points of the compass. The difference is that instead of asking politely, you conjure the spirit to appear and then force it to tell you the answers to any pertinent questions like who will win the 2.30 at Haydock and why is it that all the spirit guides are Red Indians?

Using Necromancy you can force whatever spirit you want to appear instead of hanging about hoping that someone interesting will happen to be passing your seance. This is worthwhile because it seems no-one interesting can get anywhere near a seance because of the crowd of Red Indians.

OCCULT LITERATURE

You are not supposed to read these books. That would be too much like hard work. But it is vital that you give the impression that you have read them. It is enough to know just the name and the briefest description of the contents to carry it off. For example saying "War and Peace is about Russia" shows about the right level of knowledge.

Should you feel rash enough to attempt to tackle any on the list there is a particular way to read occult literature which you would be better to know.

For a start never read the first five chapters. There are two theories why these chapters are always totally unreadable. One says that this is a form of protection to ward off the profane or casually interested, who will give up after reading four chapters of unintelligible nonsense. The other one says that the writers normally can't keep up the obscurity level and let some facts slip through by accident. You are therefore pretty safe in quoting something from chapter three or four of any of the following books as even if the first five chapters have been read, they will not have been understood.

The Book Of The Dead – A collection of Egyptian invocations and spells which were used to do the most unlikely things. It was written between 1500 B.C. and 250 B.C. which just shows that the Egyptians were very slow writers. It was created at the time when eternal life was being democratised – i.e. it was no longer just the Pharoah who got heaven. The pharoahs immediately started looking for somewhere better to go. This gave the Egyptian-in-the-street a few problems he hadn't had to face before he got a chance at eternal after-life. For instance he suddenly became very interested in spells to stop Crocodiles eating him in the Underworld.

Possibly the best sounding spell is the one 'to become Ptah, eat bread, drink beer, purify the hinder-parts and live in Heliopolis'.

The Golden Asse Of Apuleius – Often mentioned as an early classic of magical literature and a definitive study of shape-shifting. A rather banal fairy story about a witch changing a man into an ass. Not as interesting as Little Red Riding Hood and just about as informative.

It really seems to have gained popularity when its name was changed from 'The XI Bookes of the Golden Asse Conteininge the Metamorphosie of Lucius Apuleius, enterlaced With sondrie pleasaunt and delectable Tales'. So you see dyslexia was a real problem even in 1566.

Originally written in Latin and translated into English by Adlington although it is difficult to tell which is which at times, it was much admired by Crowley, presumably because he thought he was the only person with a copy.

The Key Of Solomon – This is the grimoire that is always being used by powerful Black Magicians in popular occult fiction. About the most interesting thing they could do from this is to exorcise a bat (after which you sacrifice it and collect its blood).

Most people presume that there is only one pentacle – i.e. the Pentacle or Seal of Solomon. In fact there are dozens of pentacles and *The Key* lists them in monotonous detail, along with what they do, and the names of the angels or spirits connected with them. Ideal bed-time reading.

The Key's method of making sure that you cannot

complete any exercise properly is to insist that you do everything on a day ruled by a certain planet and at an hour ruled by another planet. For example if you want to make Magic Garters you must kill a hare on the 25th of January. The 24th or 26th would be no good at all.

Magic garters, by the way, allow you to travel in any given direction at great speed – a sort of magical Porsche. If it wasn't for the problems of getting the dates right they would probably be compulsory fashion wear already.

Actions With The Spirits – Dr John Dee. This book is interesting because it is big and bound in leather. It is not what you would call a blockbuster exactly. First published in 1659 it was reprinted in a limited edition in 1974 (due only to sustained public demand). Eliphas Levi borrowed from it extensively when evolving his Ritual Magic and of course Aleister Crowley devoted a few years to it, and sorted it all out once and for all (at least as far as he was concerned). It is impossible to read due to the fact that Dr Dee seemed to be confused between the letters 'S' and 'F', but it does look impressive.

Malleus Mallificorum – The Hammer of the Witches. A handbook for witch trials and a real bestseller. It was first published in 1486, just when Torquemada was winding up to the Inquisition and every printing thereafter seemed to coincide with an outbreak of witchcraft and the resulting spate of witch trials. It was favourite reading for King James I who would read it by the light of a burning witch.

It was knocked up by a comedy duo Kramer and Sprenger, two jovial Dominican monks, and starts off pretty uncompromisingly by pointing out that to suggest that there are no such things as witches 'manifestly savours of heresy'. It is packed with interesting details like 'Whether witches may work some prestidigitary illusion so that the male organ appears to be entirely removed and separate from the body' and handy practical hints like 'Remedies prescribed for those who by prestidigitary art have lost their virile member or have seemingly been transformed into the shapes of beasts.' A must for all serious witch finders.

Qabalism – Virtually everyone has written a book on Qabalism so it is pretty safe just to say "Have you read Levi/Crowley/Waite/Blavatsky/Barbara Cartland on Qabalism?" (delete as necessary) with utmost confidence. However don't ever write this down as they all spelt the word differently.

Of course despite the fact that they all say they are writing on the same subject you wouldn't guess it to read the books so don't get into too much detail.

PARAPHERNALIA

There is nothing to enhance your reputation as an adept, than having the right paraphernalia. There are certain shops eager to sell you eyes of newt and toes of frog (size three assorted) and all those little odds and ends which give your spells that little bit extra. But beware. You can't really be sure the fillet of fenny snake is fresh and you would have to check carefully the sell-by dates on adder's fork and blind-worm sting.

If you do frequent these establishments, under no circumstances admit to it. If anyone mentions having bought anything from them, immediately point out that there is absolutely no point in buying your lizard's leg or howlet's wing as the very act of collecting these objects is part of the magical action. The objects themselves have no intrinsic value but the dedication required to bring them all together creates the atmosphere of commitment that is needed to perform the task. You can't just pop down to the supermarket and stick them on Access.

Naturally the true bluffer will feel no necessity to take his or her own advice. Buy anything you want there yourself, though don't leave it lying about the house in its original cellophane wrapping.

Wands
Magicians of old always carried a wand. In fact they wouldn't go anywhere without them, concealing them in the sleeves of their voluminous robes. It is probably more sensible now to get an attachment to fit it to your Filofax.

The wand allows the magician to concentrate his powers on to a specific place by pointing or touching. It must be said that Freud would probably have something to say about this.

A wizard's wand is always cut from hazel wood at sunrise unless of course it is for black magic when a cypress tree that grows at a cross-roads is needed. The bluffer uses any type of wood that suits, on the grounds that no-one will know the difference anyway. The medieval magician usually had a magnet fitted at one end but when the general public discovered that it wasn't magic that attracted little bits of metal to it, the style died away somewhat. Far more important are a few authentic-looking Hebrew characters scratched on it.

There are a couple of words of warning, though. Don't hand it round at the pub for everyone to see. Real magicians would never let another human being touch their wand. A Magician only used his wand rarely to conserve its power. As yours won't work at all use it even more rarely.

Swords

A sword is something that you really need to have to be a convincing ritual magic exponent. The grimoires happily tell you to forge your own and inscribe it yourself with certain astrological and qabalistic signs. Quite frankly this is a bit of a pain in the neck especially when you can buy a perfectly good one off the shelf in a magic shop.

Magicians and witches use these extensively to point at things and people (their mothers presumably never told them it was rude). If you actually come across a piece of ceremonial magic ritual that doesn't involve pointing your sword at the four points of the compass – do it anyway.

Incense

Nothing sets the atmosphere like a bit of incense burning. People expect something queer-smelling spluttering away at the corners of your magic circle. There are all sorts of different aromatics to do all sorts of unlikely things, for example: Incense For Banishing Unwanted Influences. If anyone else uses the word 'incense' always point out that it can only be used to describe the gum resin of the trees from the Boswellia family virtually only found on the Somali coast of East Africa and then point out that it should properly be called Frankincense. That should shut them up.

Candles
Naturally candles are vital for any serious magical exercise. Have as many candles as you can afford and vary the colours. There is a special branch of 'candle magic' that performs various feats by burning the correct number of correctly coloured candles in the correct lay-out. If you do this, please resist the temptation to blow them all out and sing 'Happy Birthday to You'.

The Magic Circle
To complete the set-up you must have a magic circle painted on a floor somewhere. Pull back the carpet for this – it just looks silly painted on rough shag pile. This should be at least a double circle with a lot of Hebrew and Egyptian characters, pentacles and astrological insignia dotted around. It is quite normal to draw a pentagram (a five pointed star) in the middle, but make sure it's the right way up or it becomes a sign of the Devil. What the right way up is in a circle is your problem.

THE AUTHOR

No-one seems to know when Alexander Cameron Rae was born although he has been known to let slip details of conversation that he had with Disraeli and he is known to be a life long friend of Count Cagliostro. Suffice it to say that he looks remarkably young and fresh faced.

It is thought that he knows more about his subject than he divulged in this book but it is rumoured that he is sworn to secrecy by an unnamed but extremely powerful occult group.

What is known is that he is a Scot (he still writes with a distinct Scottish accent) and he now lives in darkest Wiltshire. Since arriving in England he has assumed his family title Le Duc de Auchenshuggle.

He has made a life-long study of the occult and has impressive results reading the Tarot and using I Ching and Astrology, although he has had to give this up recently due to unforeseen circumstances. In his spare time he is a journalist. He has a wife and about two children (Attila and Ghenghis).

THE BLUFFER'S GUIDES

Available @ £1.00 each:

Accountancy	Management
Antiques	Marketing
Bluffing	Music
Class	Paris
Computers	Philosophy
Consultancy	Photography
Feminism	Publishing
Golf	Sex
Hi-Fi	Teaching
Hollywood	Television
Jazz	Theatre
Literature	Wine

Available @ £1.95 each:

Ballet
Cricket
Fortune Telling
Maths
The Occult
University

All these books are available at your local bookshop or newsagent, or can be ordered direct from the publisher. Just tick the titles you require and fill in the form below. Prices and availability subject to change without notice.

Ravette Books Limited, 3 Glenside Estate, Star Road, Partridge Green, Horsham, West Sussex RH13 8RA

Please send a cheque or postal order, and allow the following for postage and packing. UK 25p for one book and 10p for each additional book ordered.

Name...

Address..

....

THE BLUFFER'S GUIDES